THE ENEMY OF GIVING UP

Albert Chatmon, Jr.

The Enemy of Giving Up

Published by Spines

ISBN: 979-8-89383-130-6

THE ENEMY OF GIVING UP

ALBERT CHATMON JR.

Contents

Acknowledgments

I am surrounded by people who have contributed so much to my success in life. I want to express my deepest appreciation to my wife, Lashaun Chatmon; my sons, Albert and Allen Chatmon; my parents, Albert and Lydia Chatmon; my siblings, Christine and Peter Chatmon; and my best friend, Darnell Scotton. My journey would look so different, and this book would not have been possible without each one of you. Without their love and encouragement, I would have given up a long time ago.

Chapter 1

Before We Begin

I have often heard that the greatest secret of success lies within our minds.

I HAD FALLEN in love with my then-girlfriend and decided to propose to her. I purchased the engagement ring and made reservations at a really nice restaurant at the pier in Georgetown, in Washington, DC. On the day of, I got my haircut and washed my car. I previously bought a new outfit and went home to get ready for this special day.

When I arrived at my house, I sprayed the tire shine on the tires to ensure that my ride was looking perfect. Then I went inside, confirmed our date and got ready. I was so nervous that I got dressed really early. I just happened to look out of the window at my car and noticed that the tires weren't shining. I thought, wow, maybe I didn't spray it on right. So, I went back out and sprayed the tires again. This time, I made sure to cover the tires appropriately.

Then, about thirty minutes prior to my time to leave, I noticed that, once again, my tires were not shining. Now, I was beginning to get upset, considering that this was going to be my big day and that everything must go perfectly. Not today, please, any day, but this day. So, this time, I went back out, shook up the can vehemently and sprayed each tire twice. I watched carefully to make sure that the entire tire was covered with the foam and went back inside to wait a few minutes for it to dry. But it still didn't shine my tires.

I was so upset. *This is the day that I'm about to propose to my wife, and I can't get my tires to shine.* Everything was ready: the ring, the reservation was set, my outfit was sharp, and I even practiced my proposal speech, but I couldn't get my tires to shine. *Of all the days for me to have a bad can of tire shine.* I wasn't having it. So, I called up the manufacturer and reached a customer service representative. I began to explain my situation, expressing the importance of this day and why it was so important that their product work on this day. That's right, I made a big fuss and wanted them to feel my pain and frustration because their carpet cleaner was not shining my tires...

Wait, carpet cleaner? Uhm, all this time, I was shining my tires with the carpet cleaner. In my excitement, I was so focused on the dream that I overlooked and missed a small thing, such as picking up the right can. My tires were the cleanest tires on the East Coast.

Truth be told, we do this often. Maybe not with our tires, but definitely in other aspects of life. Most of the time, our focus is so much on the big picture that we miss the small pieces that make the picture great. We miss the small details that help us to reach real success.

I have often heard that the greatest secret of success lies within our minds. It's about how we think, and it's clear that successful and unsuccessful people think differently. But what if it were deeper than that?

The secrets of life seem always to be hidden from plain view and require some form of revelation. However, once discovered, it can be life-changing if applied correctly. Life, then, is full of mysteries that, if sought after, can mature and benefit us greatly. Unfortunately, most people are unaware of this and consequently never reach their full potential or real success.

Therefore, it appears that the truth about success is in discovering which mystery places us in the right direction.

I write this book to help you understand a mystery tool that helps you to be successful in any endeavor you choose. It's nothing new, just something that we sometimes overlook. You will find that each successful person understands and has applied this tool at some point to reach their success. You will also find that this mystery tool is not hard or difficult but will require a different thought process. Not understanding this secret may cost you dearly.

I have studied successful people for years and have discovered that no matter what field they were in, they always use this mystery tool. In fact, every person that I have researched in one way or the other have used this mystery tool to specifically obtain their success. From entrepreneurs dealing with great barriers in business to athletes dealing with physical or emotional challenges, they have all had to dig deep and count on this mystery tool.

I only call this a mystery tool because its value seems to be hidden from us and only revealed when faced with challenges. However, once rediscovered it becomes one of the most important tools used to obtain success. In fact, I believe that each successful person will agree that through any obstacle, it was this mystery tool that in some way helped them to become successful.

I think it's best also to say that it's not about one's aptitude, wealth, status in life, or intelligence that fully contributes to one's success. Think about those who were in poverty or suffered physical challenges, who overcame great odds to become successful. In fact, there seems to be no real cookie-cutter equation that, if followed, guarantees success. However, the equation of success includes this mystery tool. Just like for every mathematical equation, one must have the equal sign; you must include this mystery tool to reach a true level of success.

You will even notice that some successful people in life are short, while others are tall. Some are men, while others are women. Some are dark-skinned, while others are light-skinned. This does not seem to matter because, either way, we find that successful and unsuccessful people would fit into any of these categories. Even knowledge or education, although it may help, still does not guarantee success. Come to think of it; there are only a few things that really help us to obtain success or a means towards victory. If you study successful people carefully, you will find that none of these things guarantee success.

Yes, some people are born with a gift or talent that makes it easier to rise to the top. At the same time, others have to work harder to get to the same position. Yet, even the talented person must discover and use this mystery tool. Even the person with money, wealth, prestige, you name it, must, at one point or another, use this mystery tool.

Sure, thinking plays a huge role in one's success. As a matter of fact, it actually separates successful people from unsuccessful people. But a part of the process of one's success is within itself a mystery.

So then, what is the forgotten mystery tool?

CHAPTER 2

THE MYSTERY TOOL

Perseverance - persistence in doing something despite difficulty or delay in achieving success.

BEFORE I BEGIN, let me explain why I believe that perseverance is so important. Let me use three phrases that everyone is familiar with and which separate successful people from unsuccessful people. They are "giving up, giving in and quitting." And it's perseverance that is the enemy of all three.

You have heard it said that life is what you make it. In some part , I really believe that this is true. So then, why are so many people unhappy or unsatisfied in life? If life really is what we make it, then are some people actually making their own lives miserable? Unfortunately, they are.

As you can see, those who are successful in life also face some adversity. So then, it's not being without problems that determine one's success. Further, it appears that it's not even the problem but one's attitude as to how one deals with the problem that determines success.

If we dive deeper into the life of Helen Keller, who is known as an author, political activist and speaker, she too had many real challenges. We will find that she was blind, deaf and mute. How can someone with these challenges be successful in writing a book or being a speaker? Wouldn't the challenges that she faced be considered astronomical to the point where she should not be able to do this? Can you imagine being a political activist or lecturer yet unable to hear, nor can you see or speak? Yet, not only has she accomplished this, but she has reached levels of great success.

However, she is not the only person who has overcome what seems to be impossible. If you look throughout the history of man, you will find numerous individuals who have made it through impossible odds to become very successful. In contrast, you will find numerous people who have just given up. So, what is the difference? What helped Helen Keller to reach her level of success?

Things happen.

Sometimes life happens. If we think about it, when we are faced with these challenges, maybe God is urging us to get out of our box. Maybe there is success at the end of a very bumpy road.

Further, maybe the bumpy road is what makes us strong enough to handle the outcome of success. Maybe it's through the challenges that we become even wiser, better, and even develop more as mature people. Perhaps it's actually better for us to go through challenging things in life. Maybe we have been trying to avoid that which actually makes us great.

Most people take the easy road. As a matter of fact, you will find that is exactly what most people do. They start and then quit. Been there, done that. But what if circumstances were given to us to help us become better? What if the important part of life was actually going through things? What if our maturity or spiritual growth is actually connected to life's challenges? What if the secret to even becoming better is actually going through things? What if the greatest part of life is actually overlooked because of our lack of understanding of the point that challenges help us to grow? What if the process of success includes failure?

Have you ever gone through something that you just decided to make it through and not quit? What made you reach the end? Where did the decision not to quit come from? Was it made out of desperation or necessity? Or was it just because you determined you were going to reach the end?

Here is a thought: why did you continue through that but give up on other things? Something to think about,, isn't it?

Did you know that a key difference between successful and unsuccessful people starts with the fact that they didn't quit? Instead, they chose to persevere. So, if that's the case, why do we even consider giving up or quitting? Yet, we do this so often.

Another thought is that most people actually listen to and do what others say. So, if someone else says that they cannot do something, most receive and believe it. So if they listen to a quitter, even if they really can do something, they can't because they have accepted someone else's perspective instead of the truth. It's interesting because the reason you started in the first place was because you thought you could do it. So, like many others, you get started, and for some reason, when faced with challenges, you listen to others and decide to quit.

Then, there's the person who gets started, but when they are challenged by a hurdle, they decide to give up. What happened? Maybe in their mind, somehow, they found that the hurdle is bigger than they thought, or maybe the hurdle is bigger than the goal. So, why start if you are not going to finish?

I believe the difference between success and unsuccess is perseverance. Be willing to face obstacles, jump over hurdles, or do what must be done to become successful. All successful people have at least one thing in common: they persevered through something to get where they are today. Actually, most will even tell you that it was through their perseverance that they learned of an inner strength that helped them to reach their success.

This inner strength helps them to be wiser, stronger, and more persistent about being successful. There really is something about someone who has reached a true level of success. They seemed to have learned the mystery of perseverance, even when they could not see how. They chose to hang in there, move forward and make their goals and dreams come to fruition. And get this: even when others told them that they couldn't, they still believed that they could.

But most emphatically, they believed in the why and chose to persevere through the how. They focused more on the way, which overshadowed the how. It's the how thst always seems to be bigger than the dream. How can anyone be the greatest basketball player of all time after being kicked off from their High School basketball team? Or, how can someone be a great dancer with only one eye? These stars chose to overlook the how and focus on the why. It is in the why that helps us to persevere. Those who focus on the why persevere and choose not to give up, not give in or never quit. It is the inspiration of the why that incubates the characteristic of success forged through their choice of perseverance.

For most successful people, success is defined as reaching the goal. Plain and simple. Whatever the goal is, it's imperative to reach it. Therefore, the answer to obtaining success is to persevere through any obstacle to reach the goal. Sounds easy, right?

Chapter 3
The Value of Perseverance

Perseverance is just a tool; anyone can select and use it at any time.

You hear about this all the time. Different leaders or history makers seem to have faced difficult challenges and, somehow, overcame them. Each challenge was faced with an attitude of perseverance.

Wait, did you catch it? A secret tool of success is perseverance. But you know this, or do you?

It is said that you are not living if you don't have anything to die for. I've often wondered how important this thought really is. Either way, there is one thing that we do know: those who truly live seem to really be willing to die for whatever it is they believe in. (The why.) One thing is for sure: if you have something to live for, you will truly value the mystery tool of perseverance.

I needed to change the transmission fluid in my car. It seemed so easy, but because I had the wrong tool, it was very difficult. So much so that I had to take it to the dealer to get it done properly. The only difference between the dealer and me in completing the job was that they had the right tools. One difference between successful and unsuccessful people is having the right tools.

Perseverance - persistence in doing something despite its difficulty or delay in achieving success.

Perseverance is just a tool. Anyone can select and use it at any time. The dilemma is understanding that it exists and knowing when to use it. Here's what I like: it's free, and everyone qualifies to use it. Our quandary is looking past the challenge by choosing to persevere.

Perseverance is a secret that helps us to maintain the right attitude, spirit, and focus for true success. It's a constant decision to follow the plan no matter what challenge comes along. It carries one through pain, fear, discouragement, lack of faith, lies, doubt or any other challenge that may cause someone to quit. In other words, it eliminates all excuses and helps us to succeed, even through failure. It's the glue that forces us to stick with the plan.

As in most things, perseverance must be developed. I believe that we learn when and how to use it through experience. We can define it and even suggest when to pull it out, but it's through true experience that you ultimately become familiar with it and trust it.

I heard that each year, thousands of people make New Year's resolutions. However, only a small percentage actually bring them to fruition. Why is this? I believe it's because of a lack of understanding of the true value of perseverance.

Think about the times when you gave up. Why did you quit? Was it because you exhausted your resources? Or maybe you could not see the outcome and decided that it was just too much? I know because I have been there too. I think that I can speak for a lot of us, if not for all of us, that somewhere, somehow, something caused us to quit something we really wanted to do. The key is to answer why we quit.

When I think about the times that I did quit, I realize that each time I quit too early. No matter what excuse I chose to use to help my mind justify why I quit, the truth is, if I would have just persevered I believe I would have been successful. If nothing else, in my failure, I would have learned what not to do the next time around.

There was a man who, during the Gold Rush, decided to buy land in California. He purchased this land in hopes of finding gold. He mined this land for over two years and did not discover one trace of gold. He decided that he would spend just one more year mining in hopes of finding something, but unfortunately, he found nothing. So, he decided to sell the land, move back to the East Coast, and try his luck at something else.

The buyer of his land bought not just the property but also all his tools, hoping to find gold, too.

After a few months, the new owner discovered one of the largest gold nuggets in history. Unfortunately, the man who previously owned the property quit too soon. Can you imagine what would have happened to his life if he had just persevered for a few more months?

What gold nugget have you missed out on because you have decided not to persevere? What life-changing circumstances did you miss out on because you decided to give up and quit too soon? Even when times are rough, and it appears that there's no way to win, our superstars seem to persevere and not give up. How? Where do they get this idea to keep going? It seems to be the difference between winners and losers, successful people and unsuccessful people, history makers and non-history makers, or even having a fulfilled life as opposed to a miserable one. No matter who they are, it seems that they choose the tool of perseverance over everything.

So, why do so many people choose not to use the tool of perseverance?

Did you know that Abraham Lincoln lost numerous political races for office, but through his perseverance, he became a great, well-known president? We actually admire him for his accomplishments and never mention his many failures. But it's in his failures that he chose perseverance to obtain his accomplishments. What if life was actually fulfilled through our failures? What if the true secret of success was learned from perseverance?

How many times did you fall while learning to walk or ride your bike? If you are like me, you really can't recall. But I think you will remember the accomplishments of walking across the stage when receiving your diploma or degree or walking into your first apartment or home. Maybe your success has been due to your determination to persevere through the scraped knees or bumped heads. No matter how much it hurt, we got back up and guess what? Success seems to come automatically through our perseverance.

So, if we learn the lesson of persevering through little

things such as walking or riding a bike, what lessons are awaiting us through the bigger things?

CHAPTER 4

MY STORY

I think one of the hardest parts of going through my situation was the unknown.

In 2016, I noticed that my vision was blurry, so I went to an Optometrist. The doctor told me that he had seen something but had wanted to monitor things for a few months. Well, it got worse over the next couple of days, so I went to another Eye Doctor. The new Doctor recognized that something was wrong with my retina and sent me to the greatest retina specialists in the world.

My new doctor advised that we should immediately have surgery in an effort to reattach the retina to my eye and keep it from getting worse. This procedure worked, but because of the late attending to the eye there was considerable damage. You never want to lose any vision in your eye, but I felt like at least I could manage with having good sight in my left. I could still drive, read, and do anything that I needed to do. Initially, it was challenging, but I was able to cope. I got it. I was able to get the hang of living my life with just the clear vision in one eye until 2017.

On September 10, 2017, I woke up with blurred vision in my left eye. I thought it was just sleep in my eye, and I figured it would clear up as I got up, took my shower and began to start my day. I had a big day, and this was the day that I was taking my son back to school. He was attending college in Pennsylvania, and I would drive him up drop him off and drive back home.But by the time it was time to leave, my eyesight was still blurry.

We left to go to his college that afternoon, arriving just

before dawn. We had done this before, and normally, there was no traffic and a smooth trip back. Not this time. My vision was so blurry, and it was very challenging to drive back. I made it home safely, but that night, things got worse. The next day, I made an emergency appointment and discovered that the retina in my left was separating, too. I couldn't believe it; not only was I facing blindness in my right eye, but now in my left eye. How could this happen? Furthermore, why me?

We decided to have an emergency procedure to see if we could catch the separation in time. The hope was that we would be able to save as much of my vision as possible. The procedure entailed the Doctor reattaching the retina and placing oil in my eye to force the retina to reattach and heal. It was thought that it would take between 3 to 6 months for it to heal, but approximately two months later, the Doctor noticed that there was scar tissue that was causing the retina in my left eye to separate again. So, the day before Thanksgiving of 2017, we had another surgery on my left eye.

The surgery went well. The scar tissue was removed, and oil was placed back in the eye again to help the retina reattach to my eye. Every two weeks or so, I would return to the retina specialist to have him review my eye and make sure it was healing well. Unfortunately, the healing process took much longer than we thought. It took one year and four months for it to totally heal.

The hardest part was that I was no longer able to drive. The one freedom that I had prior to this incident was my independence. Prior to this, I could read a book whenever I wanted to or come or go as I pleased, but now my whole life seemed to come to a stop. As my eye was healing from the surgeries, my vision was blurred, and I found myself stumbling over things. It's crazy because sometimes I would actually stumble over the same thing two or three times. For example, our coffee table has been in the same position since we moved into our house, but now, because I couldn't see it, I could not judge where it was located. I had to learn how to count my steps or how to walk in paths around things. I couldn't even go up and down the stairs like I used to. I would actually have to learn how to count the steps before I got to a certain landing to ensure that I wouldn't slip or fall. My eyesight was so blurry that for me to even watch TV, I would almost have to sit up on the TV within 3 to 4 feet, and I still couldn't make out some things. I couldn't even see the screen on my cell phone. Yes, no sending text messages, reading my email, or even checking out the things on Facebook.

Prior to this, I actually overlooked the value of sight. I had it all of my life and even took it for granted. In fact, I'm not sure I ever noticed it or paid much attention to it because it was just always there. Until this happened. I wasn't totally blind, but my eyesight was so blurry that it was hard to denote certain things. I couldn't tell the difference between my dark blue and black suits. I couldn't even separate my black socks. I never thought that I wouldn't be able to clearly watch a football game or drive to the store.

I think one of the hardest parts of going through this situation was the unknown. First, God truly blessed me with the greatest family in the world. They did everything they could to help me and to be there for me. I also have the best Doctor in the world, and I am so grateful for what he and his staff have done for me. Together, they have helped me to face the fear of the unknown.

Perseverance, for me, is a decision not to give up and a choice to never quit. There are many scars on my legs as a direct proof of this point.

When this ordeal began, I was running my own business, pastoring a church and being the Chairman of the board for a nonprofit organization in Maryland. I had a pretty busy and good life. I was very happy about where things were going in all aspects of my life. We had just purchased our new home, and my son had just started his first year of college. So, when this occurred, it really set me back. I had big plans. I just knew that I would be able to go to my son's college football games and watch him play. I just knew that I could do great things within our church, make an impact as a board member in a nonprofit organization in our community, and be able to really invest and kick off my business. I never thought that my plans would be derailed because of a physical ailment. In fact, it never once crossed my mind.

I believe that the greatest fear one faces is the fear of the unknown. How am I supposed to operate in this condition? Will I ever be able to get back to my normal way of life? When will my eye heal? At that time, I had many unanswered questions. I think that because this was all new to me, I focused solely on the problem. I think that anyone would feel the same. After all, if you have never been through something like this, isn't it fair to conclude that surely the problem is bigger than any solution?

Now, what am I supposed to do?

Chapter 5

Cross Roads

The truth is I have very good excuses to give up, but the only person that this would hurt is me.

THERE ARE SO many people who have good excuses to quit, too. Some even have better excuses than mine or even a legitimate reason for quitting. Even greater is that they allow the excuse to become their perception, and our actions are heavily influenced by how we perceive things. But what if what we perceive to be true is actually wrong?

In my case, I perceived that eyesight was everything. If my eyesight wasn't at 100%, then I couldn't be successful. In fact, I concentrated more on the problems of not being able to see perfectly than on the solution to help me get around it. When I look back over this period of my life, I can even see where I would make up good excuses as to why I couldn't do something. Truth be told, if I had focused more on the solution or the answer, then I could have gone around the problem more easily.

Can I share a secret? I actually became wiser and stronger in finding the solution or an answer than crying over the problem. When I pulled out the tool of perseverance and decided to just hang in there and do what I could, all of a sudden, I began to see the solution. The answers seemed to be exposed within my choice to persevere.

That's it! One of the secrets to success is to find the answer or the solution to the hindrances, challenges or problems that we are facing. Sometimes, there is no book or manual, but there is always the free tool of perseverance. The mindset of perseverance gives us the right perspective. Meaning it inspires us to figure things out. Maybe we need to do something different, meet new people, attend a class or practice more, but It is in the attitude of not giving up that we become successful.

It seems to me that it takes the same amount of strength to quit as it does to persevere. In actuality, regret hurts just as much as the pain of hanging in there or not giving up. In fact, once you see the fruition of your steadfastness and perseverance, your life changes, and so does your character. It doesn't seem like it, but the weight of defeat through quitting, giving up or giving in is much more painful than that of success.

Thus, the thought that maybe I shouldn't settle for giving up or giving in to the idea of defeat. Actually, I can not even consider quitting. In fact, just like so many successful people before me, I must choose to persevere, too. Therefore, where is my toolbox?

I remember this allegory about an old American Indian tradition. The tribal warriors would take the young boy out in the woods, miles away from their home. They would explain to the young boy that in order to become a warrior, he must conquer his fears. So, when the evening comes, they place a blindfold, tie up the young boy and place him on a tree stump. Then, the warriors sing as they walk back to their homes. The goal was to see if the young boy could remain on the tree stump by himself all night. If so, then he would become a warrior.

All night, the young boy would hear different sounds, some of which were familiar to him and others that he had never heard before. Most young boys became so scared that they broke out of the ropes and ran home. But those who chose to persevere placed their fears behind them and would stay the entire night.

In the morning, the warriors would return and celebrate those who persevered and share an interesting secret. See, only some of the warriors left the young boy with the impression that he was all by himself for the entire night. However, some warriors actually stayed to protect the young boy. In fact, they would surround the young boy to personally watch over him. And the strange noises, well, it was them trying to test the young boy's courage.

I wonder if when we hear strange noises like, " You can't do that or It's too hard," knowing that it's not a familiar sound, we become scared and run too. Or do we choose to put fear behind us, believe in ourselves and persevere?

By the way, each warrior has a different level of courage, aptitude, faith etc., but those who passed the test all have one thing in common: they understood the value of perseverance. Are there any warriors left?

Each one of us will one day come to what I would like to call a "crossroad in life." This is a dramatic time in life when something will cause us to have to make a major life-changing decision. Most of us will make this choice based on our emotions, and I am not exempt.

Once diagnosed with this eye condition, I thought that I would never be able to drive again or do the same things that I did for so many years. In fact, when I would take the eye exam, it would definitely substantiate this thought. In the beginning, things were so blurry I couldn't even see the hair on my arm. If I looked at a picture on the wall, it would seem to always be crooked. I began to accept my fate and decided that I would probably be like this for the rest of my life. So, there was no need for me to try to do anything because I had a good excuse. After all, I was facing blindness.

I could give you a list of all the things that I could not do. I couldn't read a book, I couldn't watch my son play football, and I couldn't even drive to the gas station to get a bag of chips. I had scars on my legs from the times that I bumped into different things. I began to accept my fate and decided that I couldn't do anything. It seemed like the noise of what I couldn't do was much greater than the sound of what I could do. Not being able to do what I have done all my life weighs on my mind heavily, and I began to consider quitting my business, giving up pastoring and accepting disability.

There was something inside of me that said if I quit, I would pay a great price. I had this feeling that I needed to persevere and figure out how I was going to make it through all of this. For each problem, it was like God was giving me an answer. If I would just persevere. So, in order to deal with the problem of not being able to read, I got a tablet that read things for me. I was able to get a big screen and watch things more clearly on television. And, for the times that I wanted a bag of chips, there was Uber Eats. I was able to find an answer for every problem, even those that were much more serious than these. There was something that would get rid of all the noise of the challenges and allow me to hear the yes, I can.

What do you hear?

CHAPTER 6

THE VALUE IN A LESSON LEARNED

Perseverance may come at a cost, but it costs more if you give up.

So, I decided to paint the man cave. It is not a big area, but it is large enough that it would be a two-day job. I thought that I would be fancy and paint using three different colors. After some research, I decided to paint the ceiling white and the walls taupe and add an accent wall that would be Fjord blue.

I MUST SAY THAT ALTHOUGH IT TOOK ME FOUR days (remembering my eye condition), and I probably looked up the telephone number of professional painters at least three times, I did a pretty good job. The hardest part wasn't the actual job. Now, do not get me wrong, for it was hard work, but the real challenge for me was believing that I could. Even while being in the midst of the job, there were times when I thought, why am I doing this?

WHEN MY OLDEST SON WAS AROUND FOUR YEARS old, he decided that he wanted to learn how to catch the football. So, we went out back, and I took time to show him first by slowly going through the motions with him. Once he thought that he had it, we started playing catch. I walked about five feet from him and tossed the ball to him gently underhanded. The first couple of times, he couldn't catch it. Unfortunately, the third time, he ran to the ball, and it hit him in the face. He started crying, and I felt so bad.

So, I told him that it was enough for today and that we would try again another day, but he wasn't having it. He wanted to keep trying. All I could think of was that he was going to hit his face again and bust his lip or nose. Then, my wife would bust mine... But he wasn't having it. He decided that he was going to learn how to catch this football that day, and you know what? He did. And just as important, I didn't get beat up either...

My son became a warrior that day and reminded his proud Dad of what perseverance really means. A lesson learned.

Perseverance may come at a cost. For me, it costs twice as much time than expected. For my son, it was more painful than he ever thought. But success isn't free. It normally comes with lessons learned through perseverance.

This is why so many people quit, for they are simply not willing to pay the price. Most of us spend more time dreaming than actually working. Then, our dreams never become a reality but remain a well-thought-out dream.

Perseverance requires action; action must have a plan, and a plan involves paying a price. Remember, the dream is great, but the plan is everything. Success has three parts: a dream, a plan and a willingness to pay the price. You don't hear too much about the price until the challenges come.

No one ever quits during the dream stage unless they share their dream with a dream snatcher. In fact, I see that the majority of people quit during the action stage when a price is to be paid. Perseverance is a part of recognizing and paying the cost. It doesn't focus on how but rather gives a vision into the why. If you fuel your passion for something with your reason why, you will always figure out the how. Your reason why is always at the forefront.

For most of us, success is earned, and it comes with a willingness to sacrifice through the tough times. Everyone has a dream, and some even have a plan, but very few people persevere to fruition. In other words, the price of success always includes perseverance.

HISTORY IS FULL OF HEROES WHO WERE outgunned, outmanned or had some odds that were against them. Most of the time, their backs were against the wall, and they had no option but to stand and fight. There seemed to be something that was within them that caused them to persevere no matter what they faced.

In these cases, it makes sense that they chose to persevere. You might even say that they had no choice, but I would disagree. The reason they are heroes is because their success was in their choice to persevere. In most cases, we don't even recall the circumstances or actual price that was paid, but we definitely celebrate the accomplishment or victory. Somehow, once paid, we don't relish the price, but we sure enjoy the spoils of success.

One lesson is that to dream is free, but to act on it and persevere through it to fruition costs us something. But don't most good things in life also cost us? In fact, most personal growth requires at least our willingness to change our mindset. This may actually be the hardest price to pay, for we rely so much on what we see, hear or experience. But these things limit us to our box. There is much more to the world than your limited perception, anyway. It's wise to understand that there are things in life that you haven't experienced. So, you don't know everything.

A large part of personal growth is to pay the price of change. Change is one thing that you cannot stop. So, it's important to invest in accepting it and learning how to deal with it. People who learn the value and pay the price seem to automatically grow. Their growth comes in the form of different lessons that seem to follow both success and failure, which is tied to one's perseverance.

Take, for example, a student who is trying to pass a class. There will be some portions of the course that are easy, while other things are difficult. Either way, success comes from the student persevering through the entire class, even the hard things that are unfamiliar to him. If he chooses to do this, then not only will he reach his goal of passing the class, but he will also learn a few lessons on the way. One lesson is that he must open his mind and accept new ideas. Another lesson is that to successfully complete the course; he must do what it takes to persevere through the nights of study, tests and assignments. This lesson of perseverance will follow him as he chooses to take on greater challenges further in life.

A business owner shared a thought with me. His opinion was that people who had served in the military or completed college were more disciplined and had developed a unique character trait. It appeared to him that they had learned to persevere through the failing of an assignment or a class as part of their personal growth. These employees did not accept failure as an end-all but as a lesson as maybe what not to do, how to look at the outcome with a different perspective or to decide to persevere until the right idea comes along. They seem to take responsibility and actually become more successful and are more valued as leaders.

It's clear that successful people do things differently than unsuccessful people as a result of different mindsets. This is important because your behavior is a direct result of how you think. Wealthy people think about money much differently than poor people. So, if you want to be wealthy, you must think like they do. But most poor people don't want to pay the price and are unwilling to change their thinking, habits or even their choices.

People pay over $300.00 to purchase a certain famous name-brand pair of shoes. A wealthy person was asked what he thought about this. He advised that he would never pay this amount for these shoes, yet he owns a pair. Being confused, the interviewer asked how he got them. He said that the manufacturer paid for them. The interviewer went further and asked the wealthy man to explain how he got the manufacturer to buy him these shoes. The wealthy man explained that over five years, he purchased so much stock in the manufacturer that each year, the dividends paid out by the manufacturer were enough for him to purchase four pairs each year. He buys a pair for himself, his wife, and two sons for Christmas each year, using the funds he has earned from the stock that he purchased.

The interviewer wanted to know where he got this idea from. The wealthy man was shocked that the interviewer would even ask for it, and he thought that everyone thought this way, too. It's clear that, for one reason or another, most people don't. He believes that the average person is not exposed to how money works. "But here is the greatest problem," he said, "those who don't know will do nothing to get an understanding of how money really works." He went on to say, "Ignorance is possibly the greatest atrocity ever played on man."

I personally decided to share this thought with a couple of people. I told them about what I had read and encouraged them to invest in a famous shoe company. Then, a few years later, I asked them how where things were coming along with their investments. To my amazement, one started but gave up, while the other never even tried. If they would have, from my calculation (at the time of my writing this chapter), they each would have enough shares to receive a large enough dividend to purchase one pair of $200.00 shoes per year.

The wealthy man is right; ignorance is possibly the greatest atrocity ever played on man. The discovery of how to do something when faced with a problem might just be the greatest God-given gift to man. The ability to think. And, if chosen, the tool of perseverance inspires greatness.

The price of perseverance includes us doing something while waiting for our goals to come to fruition. It's during the "Do Something" stage that we figure things out. It could be that at this point, we are developing the stand firm character, which fuels the passion to hang in there no matter what and think things through.

All successful people have faced this very question, am I ready to pay the price?

Are you ready?

CHAPTER 7

THE HARD WAY

I was consumed so much with the why that I could not see the how.

I WAS RENTING an office suite that was next door to a vacant one. While being visited by another business owner whom I had known for many years, it was decided that they could use the vacant suite. After much thought and consideration, it was agreed that we could partner and lease the vacant space.

IT WAS A "WIN-WIN" FOR BOTH OF US. I ALREADY leased the first suite, and the landlord offered the second at a considerable discount, as long as it was in my name. We also thought that we could combine the entrance and employ one receptionist. When calculated, it would work out that my cost would not go up at all. So, we agreed to move forward.

THE DAY I WENT TO MEET WITH THE LANDLORD, I called the partner to make sure that they were in wholeheartedly. Then, after agreeing that they were, I met the landlord and signed the lease. We were on.

I couldn't handle the expense of both suites by myself, and I just knew that the person with whom I was partnering understood this. It seemed to be conducive for both businesses, as we would work together and share the cost of a receptionist. The partner was also getting the rent at a rate cheaper than they would pay alone. Perfect situation, at least that is what I thought.

AFTER SIGNING THE LEASE, I CALLED MY NEW partner to get a feel for when they wanted to meet to discuss moving in. I was informed that they would call me the following week. Well, they never called back. In fact, I called numerous times, and when the first month's rent came due, they were missing in action.

KNOWING THAT I HAD PLACED MY NAME ON THE lease, I went to the landlord to see if he would let me out of the lease. I explained to him what happened, but the landlord would not allow me to get out of the contract. I was now stuck with twice the expenses. The added cost of the insurance, utilities and rent of both units seemed to suffocate me, and the so-called partner wouldn't even pick up the phone.

I FOUND MYSELF FOCUSED MORE ON HOW THE business partner had done me wrong instead of figuring out how I could make it through this. I was consumed with the question of why this happened more than how I was going to persevere through this situation. Eventually, I ended up losing out on everything because I could not afford to pay for both offices.

NOW, I CAN BLAME MY BUSINESS PARTNER, MY lack of finances or any other excuse that I may choose to call upon. But the truth is, even though when faced with this great challenge, I quit. I allowed my emotions to limit my thinking, and it cost me dearly. Can you imagine where I may be today if I hung in there and did not quit?

MY CHALLENGE, SIMILAR TO MOST, WAS THE stress of dealing with the situation. What's interesting is that I gave the problem more power than the solution. If you think about it, the secret to success lies within which side of life we give the power to. The problem or the solution? That's what perseverance is all about, power and where you place it.

A PART OF PERSEVERING IS UNDERSTANDING that you can not quit. No matter how hard things get, It's important not to give up. Even if the challenge is unsurmountable, you cannot give up.

To quit means to stop, leave or cease. The rationale of such is normal because one cannot see how to make it through or to get over a hurdle. Most of the time, we take our focus off possibilities and focus primarily on the thing that is hindering us. Therefore, because we are blinded by the challenge, we never get an opportunity to see the solution. We also become so focused on our limitations that we fail to find liberation in hope. We will never grasp hope if we do not believe. So, the choice to quit, give up or give in becomes inevitable.

But, what happens when we choose to use the tool of perseverance? Perseverance helps us to see that there is no quitting. It provides us with an understanding that, somehow, we can make it. Most of the time, it requires us to get out of our box and cancel any pity parties that we may want to throw. It connects us with others who challenge us to find a way.

There was a basketball player who played professionally for approximately ten years. His dream was to win a championship. But after being unsuccessful for ten years, he decided to give up and retire. His team came so close to winning the championship a number of times but was unable to win the big one. The year after he retired, his team made it to the championship and won. His coach stated that if he was still playing, they would have easily won the game. Unfortunately, he quit one year too soon.

I WONDER WHICH CHAMPIONSHIP WE MISSED OUT on because we failed to pull out the tool of perseverance.

NOW, I'M NOT TALKING ABOUT REFOCUSING, rebalancing, or even repositioning yourself. These items are also a part of perseverance. Sometimes, you have to refocus to persevere. For example, you may have to change your focus off the problems and place it on a solution. Sometimes, repositioning yourself is the solution.

Today, we have very smart phones. They are so good that not only can we call and send text messages, but they even have Global Positioning Systems (GPS) on them, too. The best part about GPS is that it automatically recalibrates our position when we go offcourse. Keep in mind that you must be moving for the feature to work. This is similar to perseverance; it only works while you are moving. If you give up and quit, it stops.

However, if you choose the perseverance tool, something automatically recalibrates when you are going in the wrong direction. It's as if the desire to reach success forces you to refocus when you get off track. You can not reach success if you stop. Even GPS is a waste if you do not use it. So, use it and watch it provide the direction that is needed to get you to your destination.

If you choose the tool of perseverance, watch it give you the direction needed to reach your destination. In most cases, direction is all we really need. Most people quit because they just do not know what to do or where to go. Perseverance inspires you to figure out both the challenges of what to do and where to go.

Success comes when we figure it out. So, do not give up. Figure it out.

By the way, remember that in most cases, it's not about how intelligent you are; it's just a choice to persevere.

Chapter 8

Perseverance Is Produced

"Suffering produces perseverance, perseverance produces character, and character, hope."

THERE IS a passage in the Bible that says, "Not only so, but we also glory in our sufferings, because we know that suffering produces perseverance; perseverance character, and character, hope." (Romans 5:4 NIV).

DOES SUFFERING PRODUCE PERSEVERANCE?

THE AUTHOR OF THIS PASSAGE IS WELL-KNOWN and respected for his understanding of life and its relationship with the things of God. These are things that are referred to as mysteries and even noted as being hidden from the beginning. But Paul tells us that these revelations can be made clear to us through revelation in the Bible. Perseverance is one such mystery.

NOTICE THAT PAUL SAYS, "SUFFERING PRODUCES perseverance." The word produce means: to make or manufacture something from raw materials. In other words, if allowed, perseverance is forged through sufferings (trials, tests, temptations, tribulations, etc.) This means that there is a process of developing character, and it is through the tool of perseverance.

WHAT YOU BELIEVE DETERMINES HOW YOU think. It is your thinking that inspires your character and impacts your behavior. Hope then becomes a possibility, but it only comes after one addresses suffering with perseverance. I see so many examples of successful people who have persevered through so much to accomplish great things.

EACH ONE OF US WILL GO THROUGH SOMETHING. Your something may be a physical element, a lack of funds, or just our own hindrances such as laziness. It's so important to understand that even though suffering will occur, we have a choice. We can let the suffering stop us, or we can persevere right through until we reach success. So, what will you choose?

YOU SEE THIS THOUGHT IN SO MANY DIFFERENT ways and on so many levels. Pick anyone who you feel has reached any level of success, and somewhere, you will find two things: a choice that they made and some form of perseverance.

I am writing this book to share my experiences because I wanted to give up, too. I hope to encourage you not to follow in my footsteps but to choose not to give up. Now,

I realize that my failure was actually a hidden lesson that brought forth a deeper understanding of life. This book is a clear example of someone who chose not to give up but to see what happens if I persevere.

You know, this lesson actually opened my mind so that I even understood more about myself.

SEE, IT'S IN THE FALL THAT WE LEARN HOW TO walk. The act of falling inspires something inside of us to get back up. Maybe it's actually the height of standing that encourages us to get back up or inspires an intrinsic need to try again. Whatever it is, there's something inside of us that says *standing is more important than being on the ground*, so we continue to shoot for standing.

IT'S IN US FROM CHILDHOOD, THE LESSONS OF not giving up. Those who do give up will never learn to walk. So what happens to us as we grow up? What changes our minds or tricks us to think differently? Where does fear or anxiety come from? What hinders us from receiving the lesson of never giving up ? Wait, even more than that, why do we accept quitting when the whole beginning of life was about not quitting? "You can do it". Every person blessed to have good parents, a great coach or an awesome pastor has heard these words at one time or another. So, what happens? When did we stop listening? More importantly, when did we stop believing?

Unless there is something that hinders us physically, mentally or spiritually, we will just automatically evolve from crawling to walking. Everyone, no matter where they are born, seems to have this one thing in common. But what happens to us? How do we go from being someone who was willing to endeavor into something that they don't know anything about and grow into walking? Is it because, as a child, they see other people walking and desire to walk, too? Is it something that is just inherently part of our DNA?

It seems like the world tells us more about what we can not do than what we can do. What happened? Why do we accept the things that people put on us that hinder us instead of reaching out for the things that help us to be innovative? Why is it easier for us to quit or give up than it is for us to persevere, even when we know it's not right?

One thing is for sure: we can overcome anything. This is where the "hope " part of this scripture comes in. Hope can only be viewed through the eyes of those who have developed the right character. Simply put, only those with a certain thought process see the glass as being half full, and because there is hope (the half-full thought), one will choose to persevere until success is gained.

CHAPTER 9

PERSEVERANCE REMINDS US OF OUR POTENTIAL

A lion is only caged because of its potential.

I is my understanding that to break the will of an elephant, the trainer puts a ring around its leg and ties it to a tree. The elephant will tug on this and try to get free, but after a while, it will eventually give up. Then, as long as the ring is around the elephant's leg, it will believe that it can not get away. If you take the ring off, will the elephant feel it can be free?

What rings do we have around our legs that hinder us from being free? What stops us from persevering and hinders our success?

I've never been tied to a tree, but I can imagine the physical and emotional pain that is placed on the elephant. To know that you cannot go where you want to is enough to hinder most of us. What is even more sad is that if the elephant would just wait a few years, it would become strong enough to break the chain and even uproot the tree.

Most of us are discouraged by what is happening to us today. We focus on a perceived potential instead of seeing the real possibilities. If we focus on what hinders us today, then we may miss the character development that over-shadows today's challenges with tomorrow's strengths. We may miss the hidden treasure of potential.

That's why a lion is so dangerous. No matter what cage you place the lion in or how long it's there for, I seem to be always thinking about the possibility of getting out. Its hunger will cause it to always remember who it is. This is the same spirit that you will find in successful people. No matter what cage is placed around them, the hunger for success keeps them in the fight. No one really worries when the lion is in the cage. But if the cage door becomes open, watch out.

It is interesting that no matter how big or strong the cage is around the lion, there is still a certain fear that surrounds them. I believe that the primary fear of the lion isn't its size, or how big its teeth are or even its powerful muscles, but its potential.

The potential seems to always be hidden behind the problem. Most problems seem so impossible that we don't even consider the potential. And because potential isn't something that we think about often, we forget all about it. I hope that reading this book highlights the value of perseverance because it's in our perseverance that our potential is revealed and our dreams come to fruition.

Just as we fear the lion, our competition and problems should fear us. Potential means having or showing the capacity to become or develop into something. Perseverance forces you to find your potential, even if you need time to develop. Successful people are the most dangerous when they realize their potential. You are deadly, and when you choose to persevere, you will find your potential.

So, think of it like this: a dream comes to fruition when action and perseverance develop the proper revelation of your potential. Cliff notes – that success comes from persevering and discovering your true potential. Think of the many leaders who have been successful; they all have one common factor, which is that unsuccessful people don't. Do you see it? Somehow, each discovered their potential.

It may have been something big, like an idea that turned into a great invention or a lifesaving discovery, or it could have been an inner strength to persevere that saved a country. Potential plays a role in one's success, and it is discovered normally through perseverance.

A coach's number one job is to inspire individuals to reach their maximum potential. The team's success depends on each individual doing their part to win. A Pastor's job, which is routinely missed, is to recognize, inspire and develop the congregant's gifts and encourage them to believe in their potential. This may actually seem impossible, but the coach, pastor etc., must be able to recognize, inspire, and develop the individual. If the coach or the Pastor fails to see the individual potential of each player, then the team is destined for failure. In some cases, the leader can't even see their own potential, so the team is doomed right from the start. The most successful coaches or Pastors are those who have a clear plan and can see how each teammate plays a role in the success of reaching the goal.

Parents unknowingly do this all over the world each

and every day. They inspire their children to walk, tie their shoes or get good grades. But what happens as we become adults is that we don't have a coach to inspire us and to remind us that there is a possibility to be successful. Sometimes, without that reminder, even if we dream about something great, we give up because no one is there to inspire us. Thus, this book. If you learned how to crawl, then you can walk. And if you can walk, then the only thing hindering you is you. Someone needs to be reminded that they can run.

Let this book be a coach of sorts. Let it inspire you that no matter the odds, hindrances, or problems that you may face, there is always hope. If only the elephant would persevere until it grows up and develops the lion's character. If only you would allow the time to build your character for potential is around d the corner.

My wife taught me something one morning while she was teaching. She said, "The past is a great place to learn from but not a good place to live in." If we are not careful, we will allow yesterday's past experiences to hinder today's potential. That is the difference between the lion and the elephant. The lion instinctively lives for today and will not allow anything to take away its potential. Unfortunately, most elephants will eventually just accept what they learned in the past.

But every once in a while, you hear about an elephant that goes berserk. People accept this as the elephant just going crazy, but what if it just discovered its true potential and decided not to accept its circumstances or past failures? What if the elephant was just expressing its frustration of being tied up? What if the elephant persevered through its challenges and decided that it was time to change? Now, I'm not a zoologist, and I may be wrong in my thinking. But I know one thing: if the elephant accepts its fait, will it ever reach its maximum potential? Will you?

Chapter 10

I Discovered Something Good

The Enemy of Giving Up is Perseverance.

I HAVE DISCOVERED that developing the right character is so important in life. In fact, character is the essence of who we are, and it influences our behavior and impacts our success. It further determines our joy and happiness. Unhappy people share unique character traits. They seem to be selfish and short-sighted quitters who rarely succeed. Whereas happy people are more considerate of others, visionaries who focus on the bigger picture and are persevereers who are willing to risk time and money to succeed. The difference is deeper than one's aptitude; it's about one's attitude, which is always determined by character.

A TRUE LEADER OF SIGNIFICANCE HAS something that is so important to fight for that they will risk it all. I believe the saying that you really don't live until you have something to die for. You see this in so many cases in those who have dedicated their lives to a cause. From Dr. Martin Luther King, Jr. and his fight for Civil Rights to Mother Teresa and her fight for those in need, or Pres. Abraham Lincoln and his fight to keep a country unified, and people like Bill Gates, Henry Ford, and so many who wanted to change the world persevered through everything to see their dreams come to fruition.

I found what a preacher said at a funeral service to be so profound. He wondered how many people were being buried that day who did not see their dreams come to fruition. He said that there are so many who missed reaching their full potential because they did not believe in themselves, have enough faith to get started, or persevere to reach their goal.

It really does take character to reach a true level of success. The hard part is realizing and accepting change. Successful people realize, accept and take the necessary actions to change. It's within these steps that growth can be accomplished, and one's character can be cultivated. Then, one can understand and accept the action of perseverance to obtain and maintain success.

Perseverance is the final phase of building true character. In fact, the tool of perseverance is what helps to establish one's true character, which leads to success. We miss it, but it is true that one who has a unique type of character is almost automatically guaranteed to succeed.

Success is not randomly arbitrary but is actually a result of systematic choices. Once understood, these principles can be duplicated in any area of life by anyone, with perseverance being its backbone.

This book is not just about perseverance; it is more than that. See, in actuality, this book is about life. There are unique secrets that help us to become more successful in life, bring peace or joy, and do other great things to help us live. Perseverance is one of those misunderstood things that is so overlooked. I see it often; people just give up on their dreams, hopes or even on themselves, which is why I wrote this book.

I wrote this book because, in my situation, I thought about giving up, too. When my business didn't work out the way I thought it should, I decided to give up and quit. This was one of the worst decisions of my life. However, I decided that I was not going to allow my eye condition to hinder me any further. Instead, I choose to persevere. Yes, it will be challenging and hard, but I'm going to make it.

ANOTHER PRINCIPAL REASON WHY I'M WRITING this book is because I've seen numerous people give up and quit, too. Most, in my opinion, quit right before their success was about to come to fruition. Most seem to quit without even understanding the value of faith. I even believe that there is great value in not knowing your outcome. True be told, for some of us, success is scarier than failure. However, faith actually incubates hope. And it's in this hope that we choose to persevere and reach our success.

I heard about a man who decided to repair his broken lawnmower himself. Not having any experience, he did a pretty good job. Until he tried to use it to cut his grass.

After replacing the broken parts, he put the lawnmower back together seamlessly. And, when he turned on the lawnmower, it ran well. But when he started to cut the grass, he noticed that the blades weren't turning. He put everything back together, but somehow, he didn't connect the blades properly.

It's funny because the lawnmower motor ran very well, but unfortunately, it did not produce anything. I think that's how life is sometimes. We dream big and even have great intentions. We develop great ideas and will even invest in getting started, but until we connect things properly, nothing will come to fruition.

No matter how much he revved the engine, the blades did not work. I believe this is how people live their lives. They do so without connecting the small secrets that lead to success.

There are definitely a large number of examples that I can use in my book of people who have reached success through great obstacles. But why don't we talk about you? That's right, it's not over. It's never too late to decide to persevere.

What will people say about you one day? Will you be

successful, or will you miss your chance because you gave up or quit?

Perseverance is the enemy of giving up.

I believe that you can do this. Can you imagine all the great things that can be accomplished if you would just persevere? All the lives would be impacted if you just hung in there. Or all the great accomplishments that can be achieved if you just decide that you are not going to give in, give up or quit.

Perseverance is the enemy of all three.

CHAPTER 11

THE FINAL CHAPTER

Now It's Up To You

The purpose of this book

IN ALL THAT I have learned, character is so valuable. In fact, it is the essence of who we are that influences our behavior and impacts our success.

It also impacts our level of happiness. Unhappy people share unique character traits. They are selfish and short-sighted quitters who rarely succeed. Whereas happy people are more considerate of others, lookers at the bigger picture and people who choose to persevere. They are willing to risk time and money to succeed.

A true leader of any significance has something that is so important to fight for that they will risk it all to see their dream come to fruition. I believe the saying, "You really don't live until you have something to die for," is so relevant. You see this in so many cases in those who have dedicated their lives to a cause. From Dr. Martin Luther King, Jr. and his fight for Civil Rights to Mother Teresa and her fight for those in need, or Pres. Abraham Lincoln and his fight to keep a country unified. Others, such as Bill Gates, Henry Ford, and so many who wanted to change the world, persevered through everything to see their dream come to fruition.

I found what a preacher said at a funeral service to be so profound. He wondered how many people were being buried that day who did not see their dreams come to fruition. He said that there are so many who missed reaching their true potential because they did not believe in themselves, had enough faith to get started, or lacked a willingness to persevere through to reach their goal.

It really does take character to reach a true level of success. The hard part is realizing this, accepting it and making the necessary changes. Most of the time, it's within our perseverance that we figure this out.

It's now up to you. The true enemy of giving up is perseverance.

"Belief incubates faith, faith inspires action, and action changes the world,"

Albert Chatmon, Jr.

So,

Dream – desire more than.

Plan – develop a direction as to where to go.

Act - determine how.

Persevere – never give in, give up or quit.

Succeed – have the right character to achieve and watch your life soar.

About the Author

Albert Chatmon, Jr. is a multifaceted individual, serving as a speaker, coach, entrepreneur, and Senior Pastor at New Beginnings Ministry C.G.P. He is also the visionary behind A.C.M. (Albert Chatmon Ministries), which has profoundly impacted numerous lives through the transformative  "Albert Chatmon Morning Show." Renowned for his motivational prowess, Albert adeptly acquaints his audience with the fundamental principles of business and the essence of perseverance in achieving success. His notable quote, "Belief incubates faith, faith inspires action, and action changes the world," encapsulates his philosophy, inspiring others to embrace faith and take action to effect positive change.

* 9 7 9 8 8 9 3 8 3 1 3 0 6 *